D0071642

"This book helped me destroy my life. I owe everything I've lost to Janet Periat. She helped me see how easy it was to wreck my marriage, ruin my career and lose me all my friends. I'm happier than I ever have been now that I'm alone to wallow in my misery."

—Darryl Licht, now living under Highway 101 overpass

"Janet Periat's writing sucks, she sucks, this book sucks. I wish I hadn't read it. But since it made me so unhappy, I guess it works. I wonder if she owes me money..."

—Janet's ex-husband

"I don't like this book. It's terrible. This is what people actually do to ruin their lives!"

—Janet's Therapist

How to Make Your Life Suck

A Ten Step Program
in the
Art of Self-Loathing

by Janet Periat

How to Make Your Life Suck

Copyright © 2008 by Janet Periat

ISBN 978-1-4357-0884-6

Published 2008 by Janet Periat

www.JanetPeriat.com

First Edition: 2008

Printed by Lulu.com in the USA

Disclaimer:

This book is a parody of the entire self-help movement. Neither the author, publisher, editor, proofreader, distributor, janitor, nor anyone else involved in the production of this book shall be held liable for any misfortune, injury, illness, erections lasting more than four hours, dismemberment, or deaths resulting from following the "advice" contained herein. Nothing in this book should be taken seriously by anyone. Anywhere. Ever. Except this part. That is, aside from the bit about the erections lasting longer than four hours. But nothing else. Ever.

You have been warned.

Acknowledgments

I don't have any of these. I thought up this crap all on my own, no one helped me. No one supported me. No one brought me a beer. Well, the cat wharfed up a hairball next to my desk. But I don't think that technically counts. So if you're looking for some heartfelt acknowledgments, go get some other book.

Table of Contents

Introduction

CB 🔥 BO

In this age of enlightenment, it's getting harder and harder for people to hate themselves, to live unfulfilled lives, to be truly unhappy. Self-help books abound and every time you turn on the tube, Oprah Winfrey or Deepak Chopra is trying to help you overcome your pain. Self-loathing is becoming a dying art.

And let's be honest here, you want to be miserable right? Because misery loves company and you don't want to be alone, do you? Of course not. So forget relief, forget getting out of pain, this book teaches you how to revel in your misery. This book puts you in the driver's seat and on the road to despair. This book will give you the tools you need to ruin your life forever.

Remember, only you have the power to destroy your life.

So for those of you who want a crash course in pain, I guarantee you that if you follow my ten steps exactly, you will be as depressed, angry and bummed out as I am.

1

Because when you're on the bottom, there's nowhere to go but up, right?

If you answered "right", then you are in desperate need of this book. Because remember, you can always be more unhappy—it just takes a little work.

Well, you didn't think it was going to be easy, did you? No, that would make your life better and that's not what this book is about. This book teaches you the ten hard ways to make your life suck. Learning them will suck, putting them into practice will suck, the results will suck. So, read the brief instructions in the following How To Use This Book section and then you'll be ready.

So, let's go! It's time to hate life! It's time to hate yourself!

How to Use This Book

CR ✿ ßO

Each of the following chapters or steps is prefaced by a negative affirmation. Negative affirmations are a quick way to cause much internal pain. Say each of these affirmations aloud ten times to yourself before you read the rest of the chapter. They will help ready you for the upcoming lesson.

The affirmations are most effective when read aloud while sitting on a couch watching reruns of *Charlie's Angels* or *The Brady Bunch,* dressed in stained sweats and an old t-shirt before you bathe for the day. It is also helpful to accompany your recitation with the consumption of a candy bar, followed by a large soft drink (please avoid diet drinks—they are useless in attaining the proper sugar rush that is helpful for remembering lessons), followed by a bag of potato chips. If you smoke, add a cigarette in between each recitation of the negative affirmation. All of this will give you a head start on Step Five: Creating a Negative Self-Image and will speed your way to misery.

Step One:
Avoiding Accountability

෬ ☹ ෨

Negative Affirmation: They're all ruining my life.

The first principle you must learn is that nothing is ever your fault. You are never responsible for what happens to you. You are not accountable for your actions or words. You are not to blame for any of your misfortunes or actions. It is always someone else's fault. Accountability and accepting blame for your part in misfortunate or painful situations can lead to breakthroughs, understanding, self-knowledge and finally, happiness.

Which is not the goal here. The goal here is misery. Which means you must always find someone else to blame. This is easier than it sounds because there is always someone else involved with whatever we do or some outside force that affects us. And they are there for a reason—so we can have someone or something else to blame for our problems beside ourselves.

Here are some examples of people to blame:

Your parents are always a good start. After all, they were the ones who were thoughtless enough to give birth to you. Which makes them completely responsible for everything that's happened to you since you were born. Even if you're presently over seventy.

Siblings are also wonderful people to blame. It worked when you were kids, why not now?

Bosses are also high up on the list. They are in control of everything: your destiny, your paycheck and your daily working environment. Everyone hates bosses.

Friends and coworkers are also good to blame. The more time you share with the individual, the more problems you can blame on them.

However, there is one group of individuals that stand out as far as assigning blame is concerned: spouses. They're the idiots who were stupid enough to marry you in the first place. They are your ball and chain. If it weren't for them, you wouldn't have to get up in the morning. They make you go to that horrible job. They saddle you with children and make you take care of them. Without a significant other, would you have that pesky mortgage? Or life insurance? Talk about a waste of money. And I'll just bet the minivan was not your idea. No, you wanted the Lexus convertible.

Spouses force you to drink, smoke and get fat. They also bring the specter of in-laws into your life. How could you ever forgive them for that? Your spouse is the reason that you aren't rich and famous. They're the reason you can't buy that Harley. They're the ones blocking you from everything good in life.

If you are unfortunate enough to be in a good marriage or you don't have a mate, there are always outside forces to blame. The following are some good examples:

Immigrants who are stealing those vegetable-picking jobs from you.

The neighbor down the block who just put out all those cutouts of fat people bending over in their front yard.

The handicapped who stole all the good parking places.

Foreign governments that steal all the good jobs the immigrants haven't already taken from you.

The people of other ethnicities who are driving badly and generally ruining it for the people of your color.

The movie people who are responsible for everyone having sex and enjoying it.

The government is still probably one of the best targets to blame. They are taxing you into insolvency, recording your every conversation, passing laws to take your guns away from you and conspiring to test new chemical weapons on you while you sleep. That's why you can't get ahead.

If you can't blame your problems on the government or immigrants, blame the weather. It's a last ditch attempt, but it still usually works.

But above all, *never blame yourself.* Nothing that ever happens to you is your fault. Your problems are never because you refuse to re-educate yourself, open up to new possibilities, learn to communicate effectively, accept differences, learn tolerance or avoid people who torture you. It is never because you make choices from your fears. It is not your fault, no matter how much it looks that way, it can't be.

Because you are *blameless.*

Worksheet for Step One:

1. You cheated on your spouse with his/her best friend and then told all the people down at the bar. Both your spouse and the best friend found out and neither ever wants to see you again. Was this your fault?

2. You are on your way to work and drive through a local McDonald's to pick up some breakfast. You place your cup of hot coffee in between your legs and careen out of the parking lot, driving like a bat out of hell. When the coffee inevitably spills and burns your thighs, is this McDonald's fault?

3. You drank twelve shots of tequila and six beers, got into your Camaro and drove home going sixty miles an hour. When you ran a red light, you hit a pedestrian at a cross walk. Is this the pedestrian's fault?

4. You are a NBA basketball star who impregnated sixteen women in one year. Now four of them are suing for child support. Should you be held liable?

5. You left on a cross-country trip without maps, your license, food nor water, money or a full tank of gas. When you get stuck in a seldom-used back road in the middle of Nevada (because you were trying to stay off the main highways to avoid the cops) and you die of thirst,

exposure and starvation, is this the car manufacturer's fault?

Answers:

1. Of course not. Those drunken morons at the bar stabbed you in the back and anyone in your life should be prepared to share you because you are such an excellent catch.

2. You bet. Eight million dollars worth. Remember, stupidity is being rewarded big in America today. Get the right lawyer and nothing is ever your fault. Not even putting a substance in between your legs that everyone knows is supposed to be hot and then driving in rush hour traffic, which everyone knows tends to spill liquids everywhere. Still, it's not your fault. McDonald's should have known better than to actually provide a product that people wanted.

3. Of course. What was the moron pedestrian doing in a crosswalk when a drunk was driving sixty miles an hour through a red light at an intersection? Aren't pedestrians supposed to look both ways? How could you possibly be held accountable for that?

4. No way. They were lucky you deigned to sleep with them in the first place. You are a star. You deserve any woman on the planet you desire. And everyone knows that birth control is always the woman's responsibility. They were trying to entrap you. Stupid bitches.

5. Of course. If you were still alive, you should have sued their butts off for not putting road trip rules in their manuals. Stupid corporations, trying to kill all their customers. America is sure going to hell in a hand basket.

Great! How did you do? Do you feel worse? Do you feel helpless and powerless? Are all your family members ruining your life? Do you hate your spouse because they insisted you get life insurance? Are you convinced that all your problems are someone else's fault? Good. Now you're ready for Step Two.

Step Two:
Setting Unrealistic Goals and Envying Others

ርጾ ☠ ፙ

*Negative Affirmation: I never get what I want,
but everyone else does.*

Envy is a wonderful tool for making yourself miserable. So is trying to achieve goals that you could never possibly hope to attain. In this section we cover ways of increasing your jealousy of others and how to think up unrealistic goals.

First of all we will start with envy, that old standby for making us feel bad about our lives and ourselves.

First, go out and buy copies of *Fortune* or *People* or *Town and Country* magazine. Or all three. Find out what people make and study their lives. Now make comparisons to your income and lifestyle. Hate yourself for not having what they have. Know you're too stupid to achieve what they have. Know they are much happier than you.

Now go out and get copies of the catalogs from the following stores: Neiman Marcus, Saks Fifth Avenue and the Franklin Mint. Try to visit a mall or city that has a Cartier's jewelry store, Gucci, Prada or anything expensive—basically any store on Rodeo Drive in Beverly Hills. Then visit a Rolls Royce dealership and a Mercedes Benz dealership. Pick out some of the items that you can't afford. Now want them badly. Think about how you will never be able to own such marvelous luxuries. Think about how improved your life would be if you had such items.

Now think of the people that buy these things. Picture them wearing the jewels, driving the cars. Doesn't it just burn you up? Don't you loathe them for having more than you? Don't you feel bad about yourself for being so poor? Good.

Now drive to the rich neighborhoods near you and stare at the houses. Realize these are places you can never live. Realize that the inhabitants are all guaranteed fantastic lives because they can afford to be surrounded by such luxury. Remember that money always buys happiness. That the people who purchase such wonderful consumer items and live in such opulent surroundings have no problems. Think about how much more love they get because they are wealthy. Think about how many more friends they have. Think about how many more exciting things happen to them because they are loaded.

Now think about your life. So what if you have a roof over your head, food on your table, a loving wife and three great healthy children? Are you in your private jet on your way to your chalet in the Swiss Alps? No.

So what if you just published an article in a science journal, finally found love after years of searching or rescued a lost kitten today? Did you meet Bill Clinton because you could afford the twenty-two thousand dollar-a-plate dinner commemorating his affair with Monica Lewinsky? No.

So what if you have your health, you finally made your last payment on your minivan and your son won his basketball game today? This all means nothing.

The above examples fall under the category of "counting your blessings" and they don't amount to anything when you compare them to a playing a round of golf at an exclusive country club. Nothing good in your life counts unless it cost you a bundle or gets your name mentioned in the society pages. Remember that.

Doesn't it just eat away at you that everyone else has more money than you and is happier than you? Doesn't it just totally bum you out to think of those happy people jetting off to Hawaii to visit their two million dollar second homes? Yes? Good.

The next thing you need to do is to set some unrealistic goals. Unrealistic goals are any goals that will make you happy. After you have thought up some goals, give them up. They will take too much time and effort. Remember it is always better to give up now rather than

15

suffer any disappointments later. Misery is best when indulged for the duration of one's life.

Let us look at a specific example to illustrate this important point. Let's use the example of the artist's life because it is the most pathetic of all lives and easily demonstrates this most crucial principle of staying unhappy.

As an artist, you can use every rejection you receive as a sign from the universe that you are untalented and will never achieve success. It takes years of hard work to become a successful artist; whether you choose to be an actor, a sculptor, a filmmaker, a painter, a fiction writer or a photographer. Most artists suffer through years and years of rejections before they sell their work. This is a wonderful period of time.

However, if one perseveres, as so many artists are wont to do, eventually most will achieve some level of success. This is the bad part. Success only leads to happiness and fulfillment and you don't want that, do you?

So, whenever you get near to selling a piece of your work, you must sabotage those opportunities. Say the Museum calls and accepts some of your photographs from the slides you submitted to them. Don't respond. Just ignore them. Decide that your work is too advanced and will be misunderstood by the masses. Tell yourself that they don't deserve your art. Eventually, they will go away and you can be left alone to your suffering.

There are many ways to block your path to success. The best way is to not submit any of your work anywhere.

Spend hours and hours creating your art, then set the finished products on shelves to gather dust. Let them become the physical reminders of your failure. Allow yourself to stew in self-doubt and longing.

The only exception to the previous case is if you're the kind of person who feels like they don't deserve success. For these people and *only* these people, persevere; success is the only way to misery for you.

For those of you who are not artists, goal setting to achieve unhappiness may take some creativity. One way is to pick a goal that is mentally or physically impossible for you to attain.

Example: If you are over six feet tall and have poor vision, try to become a fighter pilot.

Example: If you are forty, overweight and have never danced before, audition to become a prima ballerina at a prestigious ballet company.

Example: If you have an eighth grade education, have bad grooming habits, can't read or write and have poor moral fiber, run for public office. Wait. Bad example. You may just get that job. But then again, holding a public office will probably make you miserable so go for it.

Example: If you are five feet or under, try to become a professional basketball player.

Example: If you are a lawyer, try to become a good person.

If you can't think of any physically impossible goals to set, just add limits to goals within your reach.

17

Example: You want to start jogging again? Start with a twenty-six sprint.

Example: You want to go to school to re-educate yourself when you have no previous college education? Give yourself a year to get a Ph.D.

Example: You want to do an addition to your house and you've never so much as pounded in a nail to hang a picture before? Build the entire thing yourself without any help.

Example: You want to lose weight? Go on a cruise.

The second and most important part of setting unrealistic goals is to beat yourself up when you don't complete the goal.

Example: You're a writer whose first book has been rejected. Give up and realize that you are completely untalented. Or blame the publisher and give up. (See Step One)

Example: You are taking a run for the first time in ten years and you only make it a half a block before collapse in front of the local 7-11. Tell yourself that you're a loser, pick yourself up and go in and get yourself a Big Gulp, a wrinkly hot dog that's been there since yesterday and some Milk Duds.

Example: You are trying to fix the hot water heater with no plumbing experience. After you bust that valve, let the water run all over the floor. Sit down in the massive puddle and cry because you have no mechanical knowledge because you're too stupid to comprehend it.

Envy and unrealistic goal setting are effective methods of creating a feeling of worthlessness. Hating yourself is easy when you think about how much others have that you don't.

Remember that you can never paint that picture of a lemon because you are one.

Remember the basics of this section and carry them with you: You are a loser, you will always be a loser and losers are unhappy. Always feel bad about yourself and give up all ways of trying to improve your life. It takes too much work and you won't get there, anyway.

Worksheet For Step Two:

1. Joe down the block just paid cash for a new Lexus when his stock split. It is polished, gleaming and sitting in his front driveway. Should you feel bad when your beat up, tan Ford Escort dies directly in front of his house?

2. The director of the Modern Museum of Art has seen your watercolors through your apartment's window. She calls you on the phone and tells you to give up painting. Do you stop?

3. Your brother just won the lottery. Should you speak to him at the next family gathering?

4. The Iron Man Triathlon is happening in your town and you haven't worked out in three years. Should you compete?

5. You auditioned for a Depends commercial and didn't get the job because you didn't look incontinent enough. Should you give up acting?

Answers:

1. Yes. Realize that you don't have a good car because you are a loser. And you will never have one. Don't you wish you were Joe? You can bet he sure as hell doesn't want to be you.

2. No. Attracting this kind of abuse is difficult. Your painting will obviously be a continual source of pain and disappointment in your life. Devote even more time to your art.

3. No. Not unless he gives you half. But if he gives you half, you will be a rich person and if you completed this section you will hate yourself for that reason alone. So, accept the money and hate yourself for it. And hate him for not giving it all to you.

4. Of course. And when the paramedics revive you and put you in the ambulance, savor the humiliation.

5. Yes. Or work on looking more incontinent. Both options will make you miserable.

How did you do on this section? Feel brainless and useless? Poor and depressed? Hate everyone who has more than you do? Wish the island of Hawaii would disappear off the face of the Earth? Good. You are progressing nicely.

Isn't cultivating suffering a blast? And we've only just begun. Think of what horrors await you! Joy!

Step Three:
Worry About Everything

౧ 💣 ౨

Negative Affirmation: I am dying.

Torturing yourself with lurid fantasies of negative outcomes of upcoming events and possible situations is a very effective tool in creating and sustaining pain in your life.

Will an earthquake destroy your RV garage?

Will your mother-in-law and her French poodle that thinks your leg is his mate move in with you?

Will the IRS audit you?

Will you contract an incurable disease?

Will your stupid slob of a husband stay married to you forever?

Will that second pizza make you fat?

Is your wife having an affair with a famous politician?

Will you be buried in a cheap pine box instead of a mahogany coffin?

Are your new hair plugs starting to fall out?

Did you leave that phony death threat on your boss's answering machine instead of the woman whom was having an affair with your husband?

When you robbed that bank, did you write the note demanding the cash on an envelope with your return address printed on the front?

Did you leave your baby on the bus?

As you inundate your brain with the above questions, answer a resounding "yes" to all of them. Now watch your blood pressure rise.

Excessive worrying can be used at any time to make yourself upset. The secret to effective worrying is to extrapolate out the worst-case scenario for an event or situation and convince yourself that it is the only possible outcome.

Here's an exercise to do in case you aren't good at it: Wake up at three o'clock in the morning. Try to find some part of your body that hurts. Your head is best. Convince yourself that the pain in your head is a large tumor that is spreading rapidly to other parts of your body. Or think brain aneurysm.

That horrible pain in your stomach? It wasn't the late-night anchovy, pineapple and jalapeño pizza you ate, it's stomach cancer.

The pain in your left breast? Not the new triple-D breast implants you had last week, yes, it's cancer.

Basically, take each pain you feel and convince yourself that it's an incurable disease.

Feel horrified and terrified and out of your mind with fear? Excellent.

Mysterious pains aren't the only fodder for obsessive worrying. There are many other fertile subjects deserving of negative anticipation.

Example: You're on an airplane. Will it crash and destroy your new five hundred dollar fingernail job? Yes. Will your death confirm that you were flying off to have an affair with that hottie you met in Rio last year and not going to Poughkeepsie to see your mother? Yes.

Example: You're pregnant. Will your baby be born with two heads? Yes. Will you have to get the baby a job in a sideshow? Yes. If you unlucky enough to have a baby with one head, will it look like Vice-President Dick Cheney? Yes. Will the sideshow take the baby if it looks like Dick Cheney? No, but the Executive Branch will and it's about the same thing.

Example: You are a high-profile fashion model who tried to kill your lover so your husband wouldn't find out about your affair. But he lived and reported your attempt to the police. Will you look awful in those police photos when they're splashed all over the tabloids and Internet? Yes.

Remember, the key to successful worrying is convincing yourself of the inevitability of the negative outcome. You must believe that Donald Trump is going broke and will end up moving next door to you, that your daughter is going to marry Marilyn Manson, that your husband has bought the entire season of NFL football games on pay-per-view and will be watching all of them with his buddies in your living room, that your cat will puke on your new, four-thousand-dollar, Chinese rug, that your new Versace shoes will turn out to be fakes, that you will forget to bring your cell phone to that new expensive restaurant to prove to everyone how important you are and you won't be able to annoy me, the chick who's sitting behind you, trying to enjoy a nice meal, but was worried about some asshole with a cell phone ruining my dinner, but they didn't. Thanks for wrecking my life by making me happy, you thoughtless moron.

Worksheet for Step Three:

1. You feel fine, but a mosquito bit you recently. Do you have West Nile Virus?

2. Your new hair dye turned your hair a really weird shade of blackish purple. Will your friends stop speaking to you?

3. Your cat just coughed up something that looks like his liver. Was it?

4. You have saved up all your life and have finally been able to afford a vacation in Hawaii. You are on your lanai, sipping a Mai Tai and watching whales and dolphins play in the ocean. Did you leave the stove on at home? Is your house about to burn down? Will it be a smoldering pile of ashes when you return? Is your life ruined?

5. You are informed that you have a new boss at work and it is someone you knew in the past. Will it be that guy you beat up in high school? Will it be your ex-girlfriend, the one who caught you sleeping with her sister? Or will they split the job and give it to both of them?

Answers:

1. Of course. You are just about to die. Remember that.

2. Yes. They will only be speaking *about* you, behind your back. Ridiculing you and making sure no one ever talks to you again. How dare you show your hideous new color in public? You should have shaved your head and pretended to be undergoing chemotherapy.

3. Take the cat to the vet immediately. This book is about ruining your life, not the life of your cat. Besides a good trip to the vet at three in the morning is a great way to dampen your spirits.

4. I hope you got fire insurance, because your penalty for that Hawaii vacation is losing your house. This is what you get for doing something nice for yourself. You should have known better. Idiot.

5. Start looking for a new job. They are both guaranteed to be working there, making your life miserable. They will remember every detail about their experiences with you and will share them with the rest of the office at every opportunity. Change your name and move to another state.

So, how did you do? Are you convinced that you're about to die? Are you stressed out? Is your blood pressure off the scale? I certainly hope so. All this worrying is hard work, but it will definitely pay off. And what will also pay off is when you implement Step Four.

Step Four:
Staying Close to People
Who Think There's Something
Wrong With You

Negative Affirmation: I am worth nothing
I owe everyone in my life everything I have.

Without people in your life who keep you down, you may actually begin to develop a sense of self worth. It is important to identify those who make you feel the worst about yourself and make sure that you're around them as much as possible.

First on the list could be your parents. Do they think that there's something wrong with you because you got a law degree from Harvard and then threw it all away to join a jazz band? Good. Move in with them. This will not only validate their opinion that you're worthless and stupid, but it will cause a constant source of conflict and pain in your life. If it is not possible to move in with them, see them as much as possible. Remember, they're your parents, it's never okay to break off contact with them.

If you are unlucky enough to have supportive parents, then find some other family members who think you're crackers.

If you can't find relatives who think there's something inherently wrong with you, then you need to seek out family members who think you owe them something.

How about your cousin with the negative attitude who looks like Jabba the Hutt? Start seeing her a lot and do favors for her. Borrow some money from her to make sure the strings are firmly attached. Now feel guilty. Don't you owe her a trip around town to find the best sales on paper towels? Shouldn't you visit her daily to hear her stories about how well she did in that operetta in junior high? Shouldn't you be listening with rapt attention when she regales you with tales of her latest attack of dysentery? Yes to all, is the resounding reply.

Actually, you owe her more. You shouldn't take any time for yourself, only selfish people do that. And it is not just the cousin you need to appease, you need to put *everyone in the family* ahead of your needs. Only then will you be a good person.

If you don't have any handy family members that want to play the guilt game, find some friends who will play with you. There are plenty of them out there.

Find a needy person and help them out. Help them make all their life decisions. Answer the phone when they call at three in the morning and listen attentively to their troubles with their abusive mate. Lend them money. Preferably the same money you borrowed from your cousin. Let them dominate your life and cut you off from your other friends. Listen when they inform you that aren't a good friend to them anymore. Let them rail at because you had the audacity to take a day off to be by yourself. Feel bad about what a terrible person you are and try to make it up to them.

Remember: *everyone else* on the planet has more worth than you. You are unlovable and only by surrounding yourself with needy and desperate people can you hope to redeem yourself. If you are lucky enough, maybe you will become as needy and desperate as they are.

But the best way to get close to a self-destructive relationship is to marry into one. Allow yourself to be drawn to someone who wants to change you. Assure them that you can be changed, you just need their help. You need someone who obsesses over you and your time. They need to think you're stupid and can't do anything right without their help. Have them follow you around and tell you what you're doing wrong.

Look for someone who is jealous, paranoid, deluded and mentally unstable. Someone who was abandoned time and time again in their childhood so their trust in others is damaged. Note them by their clinging and the way they

33

constant fret that you're about to leave them. For true pain, you need the person to be completely dependent on you.

Beyond the dependency, the person also has to have the ability to seek out the flaws in your character and exacerbate them. Find someone who will blame you for everything that's going wrong in their lives. Basically, find the people who have completed Chapter One of this book. Now give them all of your power.

Never get rid of any of these people. Put them ahead of all your needs.

Make sure to give up all your hobbies, everything you love, all your goals, all your time alone, all for the privilege of having them abuse you.

If possible, have children with them. This exponentially increases the misery of both your life and the lives of your children. Which will make you feel terribly guilty for years to come. What a wonderful way to spend your life!

What's great about being around abusive people is that even if you slip and start being nice to yourself, they will always be there to bring you down.

Hidden benefit: you will appear to others as a mere victim and no one will catch on to your self-destruction. You will be able to stay tortured for years!

Such agony! Such suffering!

You will be such a success as a failure! Rapture!

Worksheet For Step Four:

1. You are a single woman in a biker bar, looking for some action. A guy comes up to you and tells you that he just got out of prison on a technicality. His crime was killing his last girlfriend. Do you agree to go on a road trip with him and all the guys he met in jail?

2. You just met a new friend through your group, "Abuse Lovers". He wants to borrow four thousand dollars from you to buy some cocaine to sell. He promises to give you back your money within a month. He also wants to you to move in with him and pay his rent for a few months because his girlfriend just took off with all his money because he slept around on her. But she will be coming home from time to time because they enjoy threesomes. Do you move in with him and join their sex games?

3. Your new husband has decided you shouldn't have any friends outside of him, that the kitchen floor should be clean enough to eat off of at all times, that you should increase your hours as a waitress at the bowling alley, that sleeping more than six hours a night is a sign of sickness and if you really loved him, you'd dye your hair to look more like Julianne Moore. Do you comply with all of his demands?

4. Your brother thinks you were an idiot for leaving your abusive husband. He thinks you should give up acting and all your problems stem from the fact that you are weird and like to dye your hair colors not found in nature. Should you ask to move in with him?

5. Your best friend the contractor has decided that he has worked hard enough this lifetime and begins ripping off all of his clients. He comes over to your house everyday at four and doesn't leave until eleven. When you want to take a vacation with your wife and you can't loan him any money for pot, he tells you that you're a piece of crap and you're no sort of friend. Should you listen to him and figure out ways to make amends?

Answers:

1. Of course. He sounds like a great guy. What could be more fun than a road trip with his friends? You've always wanted to be featured on *Unsolved Mysteries*, haven't you?

2. Wow. What an opportunity. Sex, drugs and dependency, all in one shot. Jump on this one, quick.

3. I can't believe you don't know the answer to this one. He *is* your husband, isn't he? You owe him everything. He knows better than you about what's good for you. And just think, looking like Julianne Moore is going to increase your tips at the bowling alley from the Royal Flush Septic Tank Pumpers bowling team.

4. A resounding yes. You should get down on the ground and kiss his feet. Promise not to stain his sinks with your hair dye. Assure him that you're going to try to get back with Bruiser as soon as possible. Tell him that you've finally found your calling: you're giving up your acting dreams and going to become an accountant. This should make him happy.

5. You bet. Cancel that vacation and pony up the money for the poor guy's dope. Why do you insist on kicking him out every night at eleven? Ask him to move in with you. Leave your wife so you can be a better friend to him. Damn, you're selfish.

If you followed my instructions correctly, by now you should be isolated, miserable and downtrodden. Isn't it fun?

Best of all, you're not alone. You have obsessive friends helping you destroy your life. You don't need enemies anymore because your friends are *your worst enemies*. Isn't it grand? So convenient! So easy to stay depressed! Such elation!

But what's best is that you've only completed *four steps*. You've got six more to go. Just think how much worse your life is going to be!

Such ecstasy! Such bliss in pain!

Step Five:
Creating a Negative Self-Image

ଔ ☹ ଊ

Negative Affirmation: I am starting to look like Homer Simpson.

Hating the way you look is the oldest and most reliable form of self-abuse. If you can't make any of the other steps work, thinking of yourself as fat and ugly is a great way to feel rotten.

If you are unlucky enough to be thin and beautiful, your work will be a bit harder. But the job won't be impossible. Simply follow my diet/lifestyle plan and soon you won't recognize yourself. You'll be horrified to realize that the person in the mirror is you. Such fun!

If you can't stick to my diet plan and are rich, then eat at chain restaurants for breakfast, lunch and dinner and eat everything they give you. In two weeks, you'll be big as a house.

If you are overweight, you can always gain some more. Don't give up at 600 or 700 pounds; go for the Guinness Book of World Records. Make a statement.

Of course, being heavy is not a guaranteed mood-depressor; most people in America are obese these days (plus that whole "jolly fat person" phenomenon), so you must persevere. After you gain as much weight as possible, you will still have to work to be unhappy. Following my diet section is a set of instructions that—in tandem with the weight gain—should create that wonderful feeling of self-hatred, shame and humiliation you so desire.

The first step in Janet's Transformation Diet is to stop exercising and stick to the diet I've outlined here. Exercise and good diet have been found to create positive feelings both physically and mentally. So, avoid all forms of exercise, get a wheelchair and adopt the following diet:

Pre-Breakfast Snack:	• One half-pound of bacon
	• One four-egg cheese omelet
	• Four large pancakes smothered in syrup
	• Half a cube of butter
	• Pot of coffee with cream and sugar
Breakfast:	• One pound of bacon
	• One six-egg, bacon and cheese omelet
	• Six slices of buttered toast
	• Six large pancakes smothered in syrup
	• One cube of butter
	• One pot of coffee with cream and sugar
Pre-Lunch Snack:	• One 16 oz bag of Nacho Cheese Doritos
	• Three 12 oz cans of soft drinks
	• Three King-size Snickers bars
	• Three bags of Oreo Cookies
Lunch:	• Three Whoppers from Burger King
	• Three large orders of fries
	• Three large orders of onion rings
	• Three large soft drinks
	• One half-gallon of Ben and Jerry's Chubby Hubby
	• One bag of Chips Ahoy cookies

Afternoon Snack:	• One large pepperoni pizza
	• One two-liter bottle of your choice of soft drink
	• One one-pound bag of barbecued potato chips
	• One one-pound bag of snack size Milky-Ways
Dinner:	• Twelve Corndogs
	• Six baked potatoes smothered in butter, sour cream, bacon-bits and cheese
	• One 72 oz. steak
	• Two six-packs beer of your choice (no light beer)
	• One gallon of Haagen-Daz
	• One chocolate cake
	• Two one-pound bags of snack size Three Musketeers Bars
	• One one-pound bag of Peanut M & M's
After Dinner Snack:	• Three Bacon-Bacon Cheeseburgers from Jack-in-the-Box
	• Three orders of curly fries
	• Three large soft drinks
	• One family bucket of Kentucky Fried Chicken
	• One large Baskin-Robbins ice cream cake

Before you go to bed in the evening, take six or eight Tums and three tabs of chocolate Ex-Lax. Having no vegetables in the diet except for fries and the cornmeal on the corn dogs can lead to some slight intestinal discomfort.

Again, avoid all exercise. Get yourself a Lark or an electric wheelchair. You will need a bigger shower area. But I don't recommend bathing often, it can lead to a good feeling about yourself. Limit bathing to once a month.

Start smoking if you aren't already a smoker. This gives you bad breath, yellow teeth and a hacking cough. And spending all that excess money on cigarettes will make you poor. This will happily make you miserable.

After you've been on my suggested diet for a few months, you should notice some changes to your body. It is time to follow my next exercise.

1. Take a picture of yourself in a bikini (or a Speedo if you're a guy), preferably one size smaller, right after Thanksgiving dinner or a particularly large meal. Have the picture enlarged to poster-size and put it on the wall of your bedroom or whichever room you occupy the most. Maybe by now it's the kitchen.

2. On your way to McDonalds for a few dozen Quarter-Pounders with cheese, stop by and pick up some copies of magazines featuring people with "perfect" bodies. For females, try the *Sports Illustrated Swimsuit Issue* or the *Victoria's Secret Catalog*. If you are male, pick up *GQ* or *Details*, *Esquire* or *Men's Health*. Cut out the pictures of the people you think look the best.

43

3. Take the pictures of the spectacularly buff people with choice abs and put them next to the posters of you in your skimpy bathing-suit.

4. Now comes the fun part. Study the poster of yourself and the pictures of the hot people. Now make comparisons. Aren't you hideous compared to them? Don't you feel horrible about yourself? Realize that these people get far more love and great sex and money because they look great. Skinny people are all happy people, fat people are all miserable. Remember, if you really wanted to look like them, it would be easy.

Feel humiliated? Alone? Unlovable? Good.

The next step to destroying your self-esteem is an easy one. In between stuffing yourself and comparing yourself to super-models, spend as much time watching television as you can. You can't pay for this kind of negative subliminal programming. But you must avoid stations that don't have commercials. Television advertisements are the key. They sell their products by selling you anxiety. They work hard to make you feel inadequate, stupid, smelly, unattractive and undesirable. It is very important that you pay close attention to each advertisement and feel what they want you to feel.

Lucky for you, television stations work in conjunction with their sponsors to ensure their audience gets the most worry for their money. This is why they cleverly show one commercial for Jenny Craig Weight Loss programs followed by an ad from Jack-In-The-Box displaying a hamburger you would kill for. So, don't worry about thinking yourself into despondency, let the TV stations do it for you. I recommend utilizing the smoking/pigging out technique in tandem with the television to promote the most damage to your psyche.

Worksheet For Step Five:

1. Your friend wants you to join the gym with her. Do you?

2. The local Smorgasbord is having a half-off sale. Do you attend?

3. You just found out that Sara Lee cakes are much cheaper when bought in bulk. Do you order a few cases?

4. There's a *Friends* marathon on TV this weekend. Do you watch?

5. Naomi Campbell invited you to go to Hawaii with her to lie on the beach for a few days. Do you go?

Answers:

1. Of course not. Exercise releases endorphins into your brain and can alleviate stress and help with depression. Which is bad. Dump this friend. Find people like yourself who like to hang out at Sizzler's food bars. Try the taco bar, it's one of my favorites. And don't forget to ask for those extra pieces of cheese toast.

2. You bet. Try to stay as long as you can without them noticing. After finishing your fourth helping, go to the bathroom and change into another muumuu and perhaps a wig, so when you go back for a fifth serving, they won't notice. People have been known to be kicked out for staying too long and eating too much.

3. Of course. But don't just settle for a few cases, go for broke: order ten or fifteen cases. While you're waiting for them to arrive, dial up Sears and have them deliver the four extra-deep freezers you're going to need for storage.

4. A resounding yes. This will serve two purposes. You will be inundated by hundreds of commercials and you will be exposing yourself to hours of beautiful, skinny people who should make you feel fat and ugly. Helpful Hint: Place a mirror beside the TV set as you watch and wear a skimpy bathing suit for the occasion. Make sure you spend plenty of time comparing yourself to the stick figures on TV. Avoid blocking the mirror and the TV with the thirty or forty empty Domino's pizza boxes you will acquire each day for the duration of the marathon.

5. Need I even answer this question? This is a perfect opportunity to feel rotten. You will look like a beached whale next to that girl and all her friends. This is probably why she invited you, so she'd look extra good. She'll probably take every opportunity to put you down. This will be a wonderful experience. Just remember to bring extra towels with you to mop up the copious amount of sweat that will be pouring off your body. And don't hesitate to fill up on the local food: indulge in plenty of plate lunches and Loco Mocos (A Loco Moco is two eggs on a hamburger patty over rice, smothered in gravy! Yummy!). And while you're in the islands, pick up a few 5, 6 and 7X muumuus at bargain prices!

So, how are you doing now? Don't know what sex you are because you haven't seen your genitalia in months? Stuck in your apartment because you can't fit through the door? Hate your body? Hate yourself? Perfect. Give yourself a pat on the back (even though you shouldn't be able to reach it by now).

Congratulations, you are halfway through my program! You should be pretty miserable by now. But we're still not done. Just think about how much more agony there is for you to endure. How much misery awaits you. Isn't it exciting? You are going to be the most wretched person on the planet! Pure delight! Pure heaven!

Step Six:
Realize That You Can
Get It All Done Today

Cଌ ☠ ଝଠ

Negative Affirmation: I am a lazy piece of crap.

Another excellent trick for making yourself feel bad is to set unrealistic goals regarding the amount of tasks you can complete in a day. Being time pressured gives you hemorrhoids and a lovely feeling of inadequacy. And it's all so easy!

In the morning, write down a ridiculous number of tasks for your To Do list. In other words, emulate Martha Stewart.

Example:

1. Clean entire kitchen, mop floors, clean out refrigerator.

2. Work fourteen hours at job.

3. Pick up laundry at cleaners.

4. Shop at Safeway, Costco and Longs Drugs.

5. Put all shopping items away.

6. Go to therapy appointment.

7. Get estimates on addition for house.

8. Clean oil stains off of driveway.

9. Paint front fence.

10. Drain and clean pool. Refill.

11. Reorganize all closets.

12. Put kitchen spices in alphabetical order.

13. Strip and clean all floors.

14. Clean all windows and blinds.

15. Re-shingle roof.

16. Cook fourteen-course meal for family.

17. Give the dogs a bath.

18. Go to nightly yoga course.

19. Write chapter on new novel.

20. Spend quality time with children and spouse.

21. Polish brass knobs on living room lamps.

22. Pay the bills.

23. Have satisfying sex with mate.

24. Send out birthday cards to relatives.

25. Read a chapter in Managing Your Life book.

26. Change sheets on all beds.

27. Clean bathrooms.

28. Take some alone time. Take a long walk.

29. Take long, luxurious bath to relax.

30. Read a chapter in latest Sue Grafton book.

31. Watch news.

32. Get full night's sleep.

Look over your list and realize that if you were truly a worthwhile individual, you would be able to complete the tasks on the list easily and without stress. Realize that if you fail to complete any of the tasks on the list, there is something seriously wrong with you. Or if, God forbid, you don't feel like doing a bunch of stuff that day, you are a lazy, worthless and selfish person. It is important to do all the tasks well. If you don't, you are valueless.

If your normal life doesn't afford many opportunities for over-scheduling, take on some new responsibilities.

Example: You are an editor for a large publishing house. Read everything on the slush pile today. The next best seller could be amongst the countless proposals for belly-button lint art books.

Example: You are the President of the United States. Sleep with everyone on your To Screw list. All at once.

Example: You are an artist who produces many canvasses a month and also teaches Art at a local community college. Paint a mural on the sound walls along

101 from San Francisco to Los Angeles. Give yourself a month in which to complete the job.

Example: Along with your fifty-hour-a-week day job, volunteer for a local organization. Make sure the organization is understaffed. Make sure that you are the only one who knows how to use the computer.

Example: You are Martha Stewart. Clean the cooking pans you use in your show today by yourself. Also polish the driveway, correct all the thank-you notes people have sent to you, make a spring bouquet out of the dirty laundry and fold your old newspapers into swans.

Only when we are completely overwhelmed can we be truly unhappy. Over scheduling and being ignorant of our own limitations can increase our feelings of inadequacy which leads to low self-esteem. Which is a great way to feel bad about yourself. So, plan away and feel horrible! Isn't pain fun?

Worksheet For Step Six:

1. Your wife wants you to go to the Civic Light Opera with her after work. You have started to strip the paint off of the outside of the house in preparation for its new coat. You also promised the boys you'd have a couple beers with them down at the bar and watch the game with them. You also promised your son that you'd throw the ball with him that afternoon. Who should you let down?

2. It is morning and you are a CEO of a large multinational corporation and the stockholder's meeting is that afternoon. You promised your lover that you'd stop by and "see" him for lunch, you promised your husband that you'd have a late lunch with him, you need to meet with your managers in preparation for the meeting, there is a sale at Bloomingdale's and you needed to pick up that cute pair of blue Guccis, your daughter is arriving soon for Taking Your Daughter To Work Day, the chief financial officer wants the game plan for the stockholder's meeting, your secretary is out sick for the day and her replacement is brain-dead, your accountant needs you to sign your tax returns, your interior decorator is stopping by with some samples for your new living room, your mother is on the phone and wants to divorce your father and needs your advice on how to take him for all he's worth, your father is on the other line and needs your advice on how to keep your mother from taking all his money, your brother's on the line because he's upset about your parents divorce and

your sister's on the line and wants to drop the kids off for the weekend. What do you do?

3. You are a mob boss of a criminal organization. Your drug supplier needs you to fly to Bolivia for a meeting, you promised your girlfriend you'd take her to Vegas for some anniversary you didn't remember, you promised your wife you'd take her to New York to see her parents, your money launderer needs to see you immediately in the Cayman Islands, your gun supplier needs to see you in Florida, your tailor needs to take your measurements for those Italian suits you ordered, your right hand man got shot last night, your new hit squad killed the wrong person and you need to make amends to the damaged party's family, your brother put out a contract on your life and the hit is supposed to be today at the airport, the FBI has bugged your favorite restaurant and wants to talk to you about what they overheard last week and it's Take Your Son To Work Day and he's about to arrive any minute. What are your priorities?

4. You are a self-absorbed sex addict and made sixteen dates for the same night. All are beautiful models in their twenties. Which ones do you let down?

5. You are a depressed underachiever who needs to get out of bed, take a shower, brush your teeth, put on clothes, put on shoes, walk downstairs, open the front door,

bend down and get the paper, walk back inside, close the door, go into the kitchen, put the paper down on the table, walk over to the cupboard, get out the coffee maker, put water in the coffee maker, walk over to the sideboard, open the container with the coffee in it, measure some coffee out, put it in the coffee maker, plug in the coffee maker, turn on the coffee maker, go to the bread box, take out some bread, take out a slice from the package, put the piece of bread into the toaster and push down the lever. Then you need to go over and sit and wait for the toast to toast and the coffee to percolate. How do you handle all this without killing yourself?

Answers:

1. No one, you lazy, stupid piece of dirt. Finish stripping the paint, drink the beer, see the game, throw the ball and go to the opera. Idiot. Why am I wasting my time with you?

2. You're rich, you have no valid problems. This schedule is a snap. If you can't handle it, you should give all your money to me. I should have such "problems".

3. What cool problems. I wish I was a criminal. Seems like all your problems can be solved by having your brother kill you. Then you'll be really sad because you'll be dead. Objectives accomplished! (Make sure you leave this book in your will to someone who can use it.)

4. None of them. What kind of a Lothario are you if you can't sleep with sixteen women in one day and without any of them finding out about the others? You are one worthless sex addict if you can't handle this by yourself.

5. You don't need this book. I have no idea why you're even reading it. Your life already sucks. I should be so lucky.

Fantastic! How did you do? Feel overwhelmed and stressed out? Are your hemorrhoids acting up? And how's that tension headache? Throbbing? Excellent. Complete despair is right around the corner.

You are on your way to a permanent state of depression now and definitely ready for Step Seven.

Step Seven:
Squelching Your Individuality

CR ☙ ℰꙮ

Negative Affirmation: I am an aberration.

The next step in deconstructing your happiness combines two distinct principles that may, initially, seem to work at odds with one another. But stick with my plan, because the end result will create that spectacular feeling of isolation and abnormality you desire.

The first principle is the realization that you are all alone in the world. The second deals with conforming completely to an ideal that feels wrong to you. Commonalties with other humans and the celebration of the individual can lead to a feeling of being centered, a sense of well being and self love. You don't want this. You need to learn how to isolate yourself from others. You need to learn how to conform to standards you abhor. Only through the adoption of these principles will you be able to complete   your   aspirations   for   self-loathing   and unhappiness.

The first step in feeling absolutely alone is to affirm your deep-seated fears that there is something inherently wrong with you. In essence, that you are a freak.

Convince yourself that there is no one else on the planet like you. No one understands you. No one has lived a life like yours. No one has your problems. No one thinks like you do. You are a deviant. You are peculiar, odd, bizarre, weird, strange, abnormal. A mistake. A cog in the machinery that doesn't fit. A fifth wheel in society. An island unto yourself. An island that no one wants to visit, with ugly beaches, stupid inhabitants that speak a language no one understands, with trinkets no one wants to buy and bad-tasting beer.

If you are having difficulty feeling this way, put yourself in surroundings that will expedite these emotions.

Example: You are a surfer dude. Join the Police Explorers and make sure to bring a big ol' honkin' bomber of a joint to the first meeting and spark it up, man. Cool.

Example: You are an outspoken lesbian feminist. Join Pat Buchanan's supporters.

Example: You are a blue-collar guy who works in construction. Apply for membership at a tony country club.

Example: You are a member of Mensa. Go to a local watering hole and hold forth on any topic you learned in college. After you are covered in beer and spit, take the high ground. Tell them that only people with little intelligence resort to throwing things when offended. After you're done eating pavement outside the bar, go back inside and tell them all that you refuse to have a battle of wits with unarmed individuals. When you're in the ambulance riding to the hospital, tell the paramedics how to do their jobs. Never give up on being a know-it-all, no matter how many of your organs are shutting down.

Example: You are a member of the Aryan Nation. Attend a meeting of the NAACP. Voice your opinions loudly. Refuse to be quieted until everyone hears what you have to say.

Example: You are a performance artist. Do your painting-with-menstrual-blood-on-packages-of-Kellogg's cereal-while-singing-German-poetry performance as a benefit for your local fundamentalist Christian church.

Example: You are a gay musician. Move to Kansas and join the church of that nutcase preacher who protests at gay funerals. Perform your latest hit for the congregation: Hot Licks In Fort Dicks. Remember to wear protective clothing. A giant condom might do the trick.

Example: You are a heterosexual, male marine. Take a woman's studies course at the University of California at Santa Cruz.

Example: Anyone. Strive to fulfill your parent's expectations of who you should be.

Now that you're feeling weird and alienated, it's time to look that way. You need to stop wearing the clothes you normally wear and adopt a new look; one that is a one hundred and eighty degree turn away from you now. A new hairstyle, new clothes, new friends, a whole new life. One you will hate.

Example: You are the editor for Vogue. Go buy some steel-toed Doc Marten boots with metal shin guards, ripped black jeans with white skulls imprinted on them, a Pantera t-shirt and a black leather jacket. Get rid of the Hillary do, crop your hair really short and dye it black. Now get sixteen earrings in each ear and pierce your nose, tongue, nipples, belly, eyebrow and lip. Speak only in swear words and punch everyone who criticizes you.

Example: You are an undernourished actress who appears in a popular sitcom on television. Gain one pound.

Example: Anyone. Dress like your parents.

Example: You are a macho ironworker. Go out and get some dresses from a thrift store, some black panties and fishnet stockings. Don't forget the high heels. Now go to work like usual. When you wake up in the hospital, tell the doctor you want a sex change operation.

Example: You are a street punk. Dress like Newt Gingrich, talk like him, act like him.

Example: You are Newt Gingrich. You don't need this book.

With this combination of feeling absolutely alone and not recognizing yourself in the mirror, you should feel both disoriented and isolated. Which should be promoting a feeling of absolute misery. Excellent work. You should be very proud of the progress you have made. Soon, you will be the most miserable person on the planet. Revel in your pain!

Worksheet for Step Seven:

1. Your old women's group is organizing a trip on a houseboat at a local lake. Do you go?

2. You recently read a Deepak Chopra book that says that none of us are alone. That we are all apart of one another, that we are all cells of the same organism. This makes you feel connected with all peoples and to the Earth. What is wrong with this picture?

3. You attend a holiday celebration with your family. Aunt Sophie hates your new hairstyle and job and harps on you all night. Your father hates your new girlfriend and torments her all evening. Your mother hates your father and yells at him for tormenting your girlfriend. Your brother gets drunk and starts talking politics and you are diametrically opposed to his viewpoints. Do you stay for dessert?

4. Your high school reunion is coming up. Do you attend?

5. You are Newt Gingrich. Your lesbian sister wants you to help organize the Gay Pride Parade in New York City and wishes you to be co-chairman of the event. She will be the other chairperson. Do you accept?

Answers:

1. Did you even read the chapter? How stupid are you? No! That was your old group. You dump them and join a new group. Something that promotes men's values. Or anything that you hate. Or better yet, go back and read the chapter again. Sheesh. I can't believe I'm even answering this one.

2. Hello? What the hell are you doing reading a Deepak Chopra book? What are you trying to do, feel good about yourself? You need to start at the beginning of this book and start all over again. You are doing a lousy job at ruining your life. Deepak Chopra...don't get me started.

3. Of course! What a marvelous opportunity. With family like this, you almost don't need this book. Listen to them, feel isolated and alienated. Dwell on how different you are from everyone in the room. Relish the feelings that you are an alien from a distant planet. Feel removed from everyone and realize that you don't belong with any of them. Love every minute of it.

4. There is no better avenue for feeling like you got dropped into the middle of a foreign country without maps or a translator than attending your high school reunion. Study everyone there and think about your differences. Realize that this event is in actuality a microcosm of the entire world's population. Think about how alone you feel with this large group of people. Think about how weird they are and how different they are from you. Realize that you have no commonalty with them other than you all attended

the same oppressive institution years before. Realize that this is the closest you will ever be to anyone who is remotely like you. Realize that these people are the nearest thing to carbon copies of you on the planet. Make the further realization that if these assumptions are true, you are indeed hopeless. You are a mutant, a freak of nature.

5. Oh, Newtie old boy, what a golden opportunity. Not only will you be surrounded by people who dislike your politics, you will be able to do some serious in-fighting with your sister and commit political suicide all at the same time. I can't imagine a better place to feel like you're the only heterosexual conservative man left alive on the planet. Even your own people will avoid you after this one.

Feeling alone? Feel like you're a worthless aberrant speck in a giant void of an unfeeling universe? Do you feel like Dame Edna performing with the Mormon Tabernacle Choir? Excellent. Your progress is admirable. You are now ready for Step Eight.

Step Eight:
Alienating Your Loved Ones

CR ☞ ♌

*Negative Affirmation: Everyone in my life
disappoints me.*

There is no better way to create derision and unhappiness in your life than to alienate those who love you. There are many ways to accomplish this worthy goal. You can explore their worst fears and exploit them. You can accuse them of behavior of which they are not capable. You can elaborate on all their past indiscretions. But the best tool for alienating your relatives is criticism. Use this weapon liberally for best effect. There is always something they are doing wrong, i.e. not the way you'd do it. You won't be able to get rid of them unless you openly torture them.

Another excellent way of ridding yourself of loved ones is to create elaborate expectations of their behavior, ones they will inevitably not be able to meet. We call this the "double whammy" in ridding yourself of pesky loved ones. Most will play the game for a while, but once they catch on that they can never make you happy, they will eventually withdraw until you rarely see them, if ever. Which is your intended goal.

But first, let's concentrate on the most important building block of pushing people out of your life: disappointment. You only need to ask yourself some questions to conjure some delicious nuggets of resentment. Have they sent you a thank-you card for that cubic zirconia pendant you bought them from QVC? Are they wearing the neon green and orange striped sweater vest you spent hours knitting for them? Are they eating the liver and tongue sandwiches you prepared for them? Did they interrupt you when you were giving your dissertation on the fourteen best uses for hemorrhoid cream? Are they using proper pronouns? Did they give up their writing career as you suggested?

Use every holiday and get-together to make problems with your relatives. Trap them into saying something that you can use against them later. Harbor resentment. Nurture disappointments. Work hard to take compliments as insults. If there is a way to take what someone is saying against you, do it. If they are talking about someone else, try to work the conversation around to you. Point out that by talking about that other person, your relative was really talking about you. Be insulted. Get into a huff and leave the room. Tell everyone else in the family how insulted you were. Create a huge scene. One they will never forget.

The best way to assure your permanent isolation is to use a combination of techniques.

Example: Think up a list of Christmas presents you want that are very difficult if not impossible to find. When Christmas rolls around and you get the usual boring array of crap, feel let down. Read meaning into each unwanted gift. Realize they got you something you didn't want because they don't care about you. When you open an unwanted gift, make sure to let everyone know that you are disappointed. Mope and sigh. If possible, give the present to someone else in the room in front of the person who just gave it to you. Remember, if they really loved you, they would have got you those personalized cow-printed towels you wanted from Lillian Vernon. Dwell on your loss. Your Christmas is ruined because they were indifferent to your needs.

If they get you something you already have, let them know this immediately. Make sure they know you are disappointed with this superfluous gift. That you can't possibly use another one. Make them feel stupid for getting it for you in the first place. Again, if they paid enough attention to you and your possessions, they would have known that you already owned one.

If you are unlucky enough to get exactly what you wanted, make sure to find a flaw in the gift. An extra thread, a nearly imperceptible chip or dent, any tiny imperfection will do. Or use the ever-popular satisfaction block, "It's exactly what I wanted, but it's in the wrong color." There's no way out of that one.

Christmas isn't the only time to get at your relatives. Be creative. Use every contact you have with them to find ways in which they've disappointed you. Let them know in no uncertain terms how angry you are with them.

Example: You are retired. Assume that everyone has as much free time as you do, but they just don't want to spend it with you. Think about how selfish your children are. How they are always trying to avoid you by making up lies about how busy their lives are. When they visit, spend every moment letting them know how disappointed you are in them, how selfish they are. Tell them if they really loved you, they'd spend a lot more time with you.

Example: You are parents of grown children with families of their own. Assume they don't know how to do anything without your help and guidance. Give your advice freely without being asked. Paw through their closets and give critiques on their current organization schemes. Give them tips on how they can improve their skills. Stand close to them in the kitchen while they are cooking and make constant suggestions. Are they using the right knives? The right pots and pans? Is the temperature on the oven correct? Are they doing it the way you would do it?

Pontificate on all your own accomplishments and reduce their own experiences to that of small, stupid children. Let them know that you know how to do the task better. Strongly suggest that they listen to you. Always start out each sentence with "You want to know how to do that better?" And don't wait for the response. If they ignore you, sigh loudly and make clucking and tsking sound. When they finally make eye contact, shake your head and look disappointed.

If your children are as prickly as you are, you could be in for a real bonanza, a huge family feud. By some odd happenstance, if they have a small modicum of self-esteem or are as confrontational as you are, they may outwardly object to your suggestions. This is the best of all possible outcomes. This gives you the perfect opportunity to throw a fit. Verbally dismantle them. Push all their buttons. Threaten to cut them out of your will. Wave your arms, storm about the room, then stalk out in a blazing explosion of vitriol.

If you do this right, it could be the most fun you've ever had in your entire miserable life.

Special Weapon: Criticize the way they're raising your grandchildren. If possible, do this in front of your grandchildren to undermine the parent's authority. Let them know that Ted Bundy's parents raised their children that way.

Example: You are in a relationship. When your partner does something that upsets you, don't tell them. Say "nothing" in a terse tone and get more upset. When they push you for an answer, shove them away with a louder "Nothing!" When they get upset with this behavior, shout, "If you really loved me, you'd know why I was upset!" Get up and storm off into another room, preferably one with a door you can slam. Shut them out; don't let them into your thoughts. Allow yourself to be swept down into a whirlpool of pain. Realize that they are entire reason for

73

your depression. Above all, never let them know what is wrong. But be certain to let them know that it's all their fault.

Example: You are in relationship. Decide that your mate is being unfaithful. When they look at a member of the opposite sex (or if you're gay, the same sex), decide that they want to make love to this person. That they like them more than you. Allow these emotions to stew inside you. Picture your mate kissing the person in question. Allow your mind to conjure up lurid sexual fantasies about your mate and this other person. Decide that the fantasies are reality. Now comes the real fun.

Attack your mate. Chide them for their thoughtlessness and licentiousness. Yell at them in a jealous rage and break things in the house, preferably their things. Cry and pout and rant and rave at them. Don't listen to them when they deny your accusations. Accuse them of lying. Hate them for making your life so miserable.

You'll be surprised at how easy it is to start a horrid cycle in your relationship. Soon your mate will wake up and dump you. Jubilation!

Example: Your relative is telling you about their life. Cut them off and start talking about yourself. Don't let them get a word in edgewise. If they insist on telling you about what they are doing, belittle it. Tell them about six other people you know who are doing what they're doing only much better (It's best to use people your relatives know. Like Johnny down the street, Mrs. Smith from church.) Above all let them know that you think they are stupid, worthless failures.

Example: Anyone. Decide that your loved ones are stealing from you. Notice lost items. Imagine that your family members have pilfered them from you and are selling them on eBay. Get paranoid. And get really, really angry. Rail at them and threaten to call the police.

Example: Anyone. Have any of your relatives gained weight? Let them know you noticed immediately. Be critical of the clothing they are wearing. Let them know that it makes them look fatter.

Example: Remember every embarrassing moment of everyone in your family. Recount the stories at every family meal. Especially if the relative has brought a new boyfriend or girlfriend to the gathering.

Example: Your nephew just got married for the second time. Make sure to mention to his new wife how beautiful and eloquent his first wife was. How much you miss that wonderful woman. Tell her that no one thinks that this new marriage will last.

Example: Anyone. Tell the same stories repeatedly over and over and over to the same people. When they try to cut you off, talk over them. If you can't remember all your old boring stories, tell your relatives about any latest trip to the hospital. Or your latest attack of diarrhea. Make sure to give them details that will make them nauseous. Tip: make sure the stories involve copious amounts of bodily fluids. If you had pictures taken of your colon during your recent colonoscopy, show these during dinner. If you haven't had any good operations lately, brag about your accomplishments. Portray yourself as the hero of the moment when you saved the entire office from the giant rat as it attacked the discarded doughnuts in the wastebasket. Remember, no one has made as many sales as you did in the fifties, no one is as smart or as valiant as you are.

The basic principles of this chapter are creating disappointments in your loved ones and communicating that disappointment to them. You can't have one without the other or the feelings are useless. You must let everyone know how upset you are and what a low opinion you have of them. And if you can't do that, gross them out with stories of your recent hysterectomy or penile implant operation. That should get rid of them.

Be diligent. Don't let your feelings get in the way of your abuse. You can have fun and get rid of your relatives, all at the same time. Be creative. Every time you see them, think up new ways to upset them. Remember, if they really loved you, they wouldn't be doing what they are doing. So go after them, and have a great time! Soon you will be all alone with your television and QVC. What joy you will find in isolation! Finally, you'll be free to wallow in your despair! Absolute paradise!

Worksheet For Step Eight:

1. Your husband got you exactly what you wanted for Christmas, a two-carat diamond ring. It is beautiful. Does this mean he is cheating on you?

2. Your son cannot fly out for Thanksgiving because his wife has had an attack of appendicitis and is in the hospital having surgery. Should you be upset with him?

3. You are the overweight grandmother of six grandsons and four granddaughters. They are all present at your birthday dinner. You hate their mothers, who could not make the engagement, because they are much skinnier than you. You also just had a particularly nasty hysterectomy where they had to take "three pitcherfuls" of fluid out of you. Do you describe this in detail during the dinner hour, given the fact that you are serving Chicken Cacciatore? Furthermore, do you pontificate on the fact that you find that "fat is beautiful" and launch a verbal attack on all the "skinny bitches" of the world knowing that the references to the children's mothers won't be lost on them?

4. Your plumber son has agreed to fix your hot water heater. Although you have no background in plumbing, you stand by his side and make criticisms of his work. You suggest methods of better techniques to use, different tools

he should be trying. Should you be upset when he gets mad at you?

5. Your daughter wants to talk to you about her relationship with her husband. She is seeking advice on how to approach him on a delicate matter. You want to talk about the most recent dog show you attended and the knitting projects you are thinking about doing. Do you talk or listen to her?

Answers:

1. Most definitely. And she's got bigger breasts than you. Yes, this stupid diamond ring is what you wanted, but does it have flaws in it? There must be one, look for it. Did he forget to engrave it? How thoughtless he was to buy such an expensive gift when you're still in debt and trying to save for retirement. Is he this stupid? Why are you with this guy? Not only is he cheating on you, he's trying to ruin your life. Punish him by not speaking to him and above all, don't let him know what's wrong, just cry and hold it all in. For the rest of the marriage.

2. Of course. What a selfish little creep. Doesn't he realize that you raised him? That you suffered so that he could grow up and get married? That without you, he wouldn't even be alive? What an ungrateful brat. Not only would I be upset with him, I wouldn't speak to him for at least a year. And you can forget buying him Christmas presents. Can you imagine? Choosing his wife's health over spending time with you? What a thoughtless and self-centered man. I would hold this against him for the rest of his life.

3. Oh, yes. Bravo for such a coup de grace. Imagine, grossing them out and attacking their mother in the same dinner. And who could miss the correlation between the "three pitcherfuls of fluid" and the Chicken Cacciatore you are serving. Brilliant. Absolutely brilliant. Excellent performance.

4. What a thoughtless son. Of course you should be upset. How dare he not bow to your experience? How could he ignore your suggestions? You are much smarter than he is and better at everything because you are his father. I would feel very put out. I suggest a lot of moping and pouting.

5. You get hardly any time with the girl and she wants your advice? She wants you to listen to her? She is so selfish. Her problems, her situation, botheration. Damn, your husband won't listen to you about the dog show, your best friend doesn't like dogs, so force that child to listen to you. Bowl her over, belittle her problems and continue talking in a nonstop stream about the various breeds of dogs you saw and about that orange and green shawl you're planning on knitting for the church bazaar. Don't let her get a word in edgewise.

Is everyone avoiding you now? Are people not speaking to you? Is everyone angry with you? Good. You are successfully pushing people out of your life. This should be providing you with some lovely feelings of abandonment and isolation.

But if you think your life sucks now, just wait. All you've got is two more steps to ultimate hell. What bliss there is in despair! Elation!

Step Nine:
Creating Drama

ೕ ☹ ೖ

Negative Affirmation: My life is boring.

In order to keep chaos in your negative and dismal life, you need to have a constant influx of drama, crises and disturbances. And by drama, I don't mean getting a bunch of friends together and putting on a play like "Our Town". I mean it's time to create some emotional upheaval by engaging in some destructive activities.

But I warn you, this "unhappy tool" of creating drama in your life is a dangerous one, so use it with caution. Too much drama and you could wind up dead. Which indeed is sad and dismal, but you won't be alive to enjoy your misery. In order to fully understand and appreciate melancholia, it must be enjoyed alive. So watch how you use this step, it is one of the most powerful.

For this step, you must find others who want to be as miserable as you. This shouldn't be too hard. The world is full of them.

To keep a constant flow of "action" in your life you must engage in some quasi-dangerous activities. Some of them will start off wickedly fun, then end up causing you so much pain, you will be surprised that you aren't bleeding internally. Others are more mundane and keep a more or less constant level of pain in your life. Some will be just plain stupid, painful from beginning to end. I suggest the wickedly fun ones first. At least you will have the illusion of pleasure with your pain.

The wickedly fun drama in which you need to engage is cheating on your partner. If you don't have one, get one. Then cheat on them. If you can't get into a relationship, then have an affair with a married person. Just as long as one person in the illicit relationship is married, this should be sufficient fuel for the pain fire.

The best person to have an affair with is your boss at work. This will create not only strife in your home life, but also strife in your working life, which is a double whammy that is most horribly enjoyable. If it is at all possible, make sure the affair results in a pregnancy. There is no greater chasm between married partners than if one cheats and gets someone pregnant or gets pregnant themselves. This is especially important if you are a woman. Again, if at all possible, avoid an abortion. Having the baby will increase chances for a lot more pain later on.

To take the pregnancy angle to an even greater height of drama is to have two families at once. This rates much higher on the drama scale, because it involves so many more people and secrets. Mostly this is a male-only domain, females have a much harder time hiding pregnancies. But I'm sure, given enough ingenuity, women could accomplish this very difficult feat.

Outside of affairs, the next best thing is to go on an "honesty" kick. This will make you appear honorable on the outside while you are actually wielding one of the nastiest weapons humans possess, "the honesty sword". Believe me, this will cut deep into the hearts of your victims.

Example: Tell your mother-in-law exactly what you think of her. Tell her you are doing this to "clear the air" and "get some things off your chest" to "bring you closer together." Of course, this couldn't be further from the truth, you are actually going to be driving a permanent, titanium-reinforced wedge between the two of you. Which will bring more swirling tornadoes of hell into your life than you can possibly imagine. You will be ruining all future holidays, all birthdays. Every family party will forever bear the fetid tinge of "honesty". If you are lucky, she will respond in kind. Which will create a cycle of disasters of biblical proportions. Your own personal family apocalypse. Cool, huh?

This "honesty" tool is useful in almost all personal relationships. Make sure to use it on friends you've known for a long time. This enables you to use all the abuse you doled out on each other during your teenage years to the present.

Spouses shouldn't be spared from the "honesty bombs". Here are some suggestions. Remember, honesty bombs don't necessarily have to be true.

- *I've always hated that shirt.*

- *The diamond ring you got me looks fake.*

- *You're fat, that's why I don't want to sleep with you anymore.*

- *I lied about our son's paternity.*

- *I killed your ex-girlfriend and pretended to be her friend to get close you, that's how I got you to go out with me.*

- *I'm having an affair with my boss. (See above.)*

- *I'd rather have beer with the boys than come home to you.*

- *I married you because I figured you were my last chance.*

- *My cat ate your law degree.*

- *That diamond ring I got you is fake.*

- *I have another family and several children living in the next town. (See above.)*

If you think the above suggestions are too severe, try something more mundane, something less obvious. You don't want to tip your hand too early in the game. Remember, you need to make the pain last. So try something that, on the onset, looks positive. Something you might actually get support and approval for initially.

Example: Go into business with an old friend. Make sure it's an old friend who has betrayed you. This can be in the form of wimping out on a deal, stabbing you in the back, lying to you or sleeping with your old girlfriend or boyfriend. Remember that old saying, "Fool me once, shame on you, fool me twice, shame on me"? These are the people you are looking for. Find a business that neither of you knows much about. Make sure you put up most of the money, let them owe you the rest. If you can find people you've loaned money to in the past and who have never repaid you, all the better. This will create problems upon problems, will involve the IRS, the court system and a pile of paperwork as tall as the Washington Monument. A one-way trip to hell and so much fun!

Other drama to create in your life may involve criminal activities. But remember, in order to get the most out of criminal activities, you must get caught for your crime. You need the court system involved. You need everyone in your life to find out about your embarrassing transgression. If at all possible, you need your picture splashed across the front page of the local newspaper.

A crime like embezzling from your boss is good. Basically, any kind of white-collar crimes will work, from insurance fraud to forging checks. But they must result in your capture and prosecution. Leave a trail of clues large enough to be visible from outer space. The crimes need to provide you with a jail sentence and certain public humiliation. Public drunkenness is good. When the police officers come to arrest you, call them bad names and resist arrest. They love that. Or try taking your clothes off and dancing on the table in a fancy restaurant. This will surely result in some marvelous shame.

There are many other ways to create drama other than with criminal activities, sometimes they just take a little imagination.

Example: Get caught in a lie. Anywhere, anytime, with anyone close to you. This is always good. Especially if you plan a future with the person. You have already eroded their trust. What a marvelous basis for a relationship that can cause agony for years to come.

Example: If you are in love with one person, doubt that love and fall in love with someone else. Try to love them both equally. You don't even have to sleep with them to cause some luscious pain in your life.

Example: Fake an illness. But do it poorly. This falls under getting caught in lies, but adds another element of drama. It ensures the people around you think you are mentally unstable and stupid.

Example: Skip out of work to go to a ball game. This only works if the game is televised and you are shown in the crowd. Tip: if you see a roving reporter, jump up and down behind him/her and shout "Hi Mom!"

Example: Sue someone. Litigation is good for a lot of drama. Make sure your suit is frivolous enough to make you look stupid, but serious enough to get into court. Like suing your neighbor for putting cutouts of fat people bending over in their yard. Or suing Michael Bolton for making you cry with one of his songs you heard on the radio while driving which temporarily blinded you causing you to swerve into a line of parked cars.

There are certain kinds of occupations that easily lend themselves to conspicuous and embarrassing dramas.

Example: You are a public official. Propose a controversial bill such as voting rights for illegal immigrants. Or free drugs to drug addicts. Or an end to the Republican Party. Or you can always just get caught in a lie. *No, I didn't bug the opposition's headquarters.* Get caught having an affair. Better yet, get caught having an affair and lie about it to the American people on national television. Look what that did for Bill Clinton. Talk about attention and drama.

Saying stupid things on camera is good. Like every word George W. Bush has ever uttered in front of a news camera or to newspaper reporter.

Example: You are a popular actor or singer. This pretty much ensures a drama-filled life. Almost everything you do will be noticed by the paparazzi. Doing drugs in public is good. Shaving your head, wearing short skirts with no underwear and neglecting your children has worked for Britney Spears. If you're a popular male heartthrob, make sure you get caught in your car getting a blowjob by a transsexual. Anything that the media will pick up and scandalize is what you want.

As you can see, there are many ways to create drama in your life. I'm sure you have plenty of ideas of your own on how to accomplish this worthy goal. Just as long as you keep stirring things up, you should be happily rewarded with enough chaos and problems to keep you tormented for years to come. Spectacular fun! Ceaseless joy!

Worksheet For Step Nine:

1. You hate the boss's wife. She is a vapid, self-centered idiot who dresses like a whore. Should you share this opinion at the company Christmas party?

2. You love your husband but are bored with him. Should you sleep with his brother?

3. You notice that your two front tires are bald right before you set off on the family vacation. You are headed two states away to Yellowstone Park. Should you change the tires or challenge fate and head off with them just the way they are?

4. You are a married, male, high-level politician with six children. You accidentally killed your girlfriend by suffocating her when you tried to put out the fire in her hair caused by an explosion when you two were freebasing some cocaine. You are up for re-election in three months. Do you call the police and explain the situation to them or do you attempt to cover it up?

5. You have embezzled one million dollars from your boss, a man you have been having an affair with for ten years. You have had two children with this man and his wife does not know. His wife is your sister. He is also having an affair with another woman and has a child with

her. She is your cousin. There is a family party coming up and no one but you is privy to this wonderful cache of secrets. Should you break your long silence on all of these marvelous indiscretions?

Answers:

1. You bet. But my suggestion is to tell everyone there separately. Work your way through the entire party until you culminate your performance with the boss's wife. Work yourself into an indignant rage, accuse her of shaming the business and undermining all your hard work. Throw a glass of champagne in her face for good measure. Yes, you will probably lose your job, but what better drama than to face Christmas without a job and without a recommendation for a new one. Talk about burning your bridges, you just nuked yours, honey. Perfect job, absolutely flawless.

2. Of course. But make sure to do it during a family party, like Thanksgiving. Right as people are starting to leave, drag him off to the bedroom where everyone has put their coats, throw him on top of the pile and have your way with him. Keep him there long enough for his mother to come in and find you. Her screams of terror should bring in the rest of the clan. What fun!

3. Challenge fate, honey, challenge fate. And leave your cell phone at home. What better way to ruin a vacation than by getting stuck in the middle of Idaho or some other desolate state with a car full of screaming kids and an angry spouse? Too bad most places have those emergency call boxes. But maybe if you take some back roads, that will increase your chances of avoiding rescue.

4. Oh, cover it up, by all means, but make sure you leave enough evidence so even the stupidest rookie

detective could link the crime to you. It is much better to get caught covering up a heinous and idiotic crime than it is to confess right after it happens. Besides, it was an accident, the only thing you'd go to jail for was the cocaine. If you try to cover it up, it will look like murder and will do extensive permanent damage to you and your career. You could even wind up in jail for the rest of your life. What a blast!

5. First of all, kudos to you on such a wonderfully twisted set of circumstances. Man, are you good. I think a family party is the perfect setting for such a weighty honesty bomb. You have definitely graduated to the nuclear level of honesty bombs. Just make sure everyone has had enough to drink so that all of their reactions will be overblown. Boy, don't I wish I could be a fly on the wall of that party. Really, I am very impressed with this set up. Good going!

Are you feeling lonely in your jail cell? Has your husband stopped speaking to you? Are you freezing your butt off because you're now living on the streets? Have you gotten cut out of the family will yet? Are you unemployable? I hope so. If you followed my advice on this chapter, your life should be in the dumps by now. Congratulations on such hard work, your life must be utterly painful now. Isn't it a lovely feeling? You should be proud of yourself. Now there is only one final nail to drive into your coffin. You are finally ready for Step Ten, the last step in completely and permanently ruining your life.

Step Ten:
Developing an Addiction

CB ☠ ೞ

Negative Affirmation: Drugs are my way out.

In order to put the icing on the cake of your horrible life, you need to become addicted to something dangerous. Either a substance or actions that are self-destructive. Whether it be alcohol, drugs, cigarettes, sex or food, you must choose an addiction and stick with it. Addictions are marvelous because they provide you with a constant source of misery.

I highly recommend getting addicted to drugs. This one is the best because it is illegal. Not only can you do physical and emotional damage to yourself, you can also be thrown in jail. Which is a wonderful added benefit of your addiction. You will feel miserable and humiliated for landing in jail and on top of that, you get to go through withdrawals! Oh, what a wonderful world of pain awaits you!

Cocaine is one of the best drugs for addiction purposes. Heroin has the best reputation, but I don't recommend it for an addiction choice because it is so boring. It simply won't last as long as a cocaine addiction because it's likely to kill you faster. Heroin is a drug that is good if you feel like wasting away alone somewhere. Cocaine is a social drug. It gets you out there and let's everyone know you've got a one-way ticket to hell. Longer addiction, more pain. And heroin isn't exactly the kind of drug that makes you want to go out and cause trouble. Cocaine gives you energy, it promotes bar fights. Heroin turns you into a lifeless slug. That's why cocaine is such a perfect addiction if you're a serious misery seeker. It's harder to kill yourself with cocaine, which can be a downside, but its high cost gives it the boost over heroin. It's so expensive! Added benefit: the high makes you want to sell your mother for another line or another rock. The craving for cocaine has drained more bank accounts and ruined more financial histories than playing the stock market. So, this is the drug you want to get your hands on. Go for it!

Marijuana is a lame addiction. Avoid this drug. It doesn't do enough to you. Yes, some people get completely unmotivated, quit work, move into their parent's garages and become human snails. But unfortunately, it's not guaranteed to have that effect on you. Sometimes it makes you more creative and inspires you to draw pictures on your old Volkswagen. And a little goes a long way, it's not going to affect your finances that much unless you "wake and bake" and smoke it all day. Yes, you may gain some weight by getting the munchies, but still, it's not guaranteed. So, avoid it, it's not going to make you miserable enough.

Alcohol is cool. This is a great drug to get addicted to. The only downside is that it is legal. Since you don't want to be confused with a social drinker, you will have to be devoted to make it into the ranks of the desperate alcoholic. You will have to drink before you go to work, at work, during lunch, after lunch, basically you have to drink all day. And skip beer for God's sake, that just doesn't have enough alcohol in it, go straight for the hard stuff. And avoid fortified wines, they are pathetic. Really, trust me, you need hard alcohol. And lots of it.

Alcohol is good because it makes you think you can drive better, sing better, make love better. And it makes you very belligerent. You are much more likely to start fights and create disturbances if you're drunk. And it is so easy to obtain, you will have no problem finding an endless supply. If you frequent bars, the money will be sucked out of your wallet at an alarming rate. So, go out and get that addiction and enjoy! Soon, you should lose all your loved ones, your self-esteem and your will to survive. Joy!

According to the latest statistics, methamphetamines are involved in about eighty percent of crimes committed in this country. So, guess what? This is the number one choice for self-destruction. This drug will hurt you the most. It turns you into a complete jerk, makes you angry, irritated, aggressive and keeps you up for days on end. And it permanently damages your brain! For an upper, it's not as effective for draining your bank account as cocaine (a little goes a long way), but while you're high, you're one of the worst creeps on the planet. You are sure to drive friends away. It will also delude you into committing crimes. Warning: if you get addicted to it and stop suddenly, it can kill you, so be careful. Make sure you always have enough, you don't want to die suddenly and ruin your horrible life. Remember, miserable lives are best enjoyed while alive.

There are many new designer drugs, but most are not addictive enough. LSD, Ecstasy, GHB, Special K and the like don't normally promote addiction. They just don't pack the wallop that cocaine, heroin, alcohol and methamphetamines do. But, they are illegal, which is good. Sometimes, if the drugs are strong enough, you can overdose and wind up in an institution. Which is bad because you won't be aware of how miserable you are. So, forget taking them. The best thing to do is to buy the drugs and carry them around with you at all times. That way, when you get arrested for public drunkenness, you will face stiffer penalties.

If you are opposed to doing drugs (which is both good and bad), try something like gambling. A gambling addiction works like a black hole; sucking everything into its swirling, dark center, from your finances to your friends. If you're still married at this point, gambling will take care of that as well. Say good-bye to your spouse!

Added Bonus: Not only will you spend your every last dime, but because of your exposure to all that second hand smoke, you also might get lung cancer! Could it get any better? Yes! It's also a place where you are served free alcohol, your reward from the casino for flushing your life down the toilet. So not only can you be addicted to gambling, you can be addicted to alcohol all at the same time! A great combination addiction! Absolute rapture!

Okay, so, you're not much of a gambler or a drinker. And you really hate drugs. Try a sex addiction. It's fun and destructive. For males there is the added benefit of the difficulty of getting laid. Most men have to get married to assure themselves a constant source of sex (but that's no guarantee as most married men will attest). A single man with a sex addiction can be a very lonely, sorrowful man. Exactly what you're looking for: Desperation and unmet need all in one shot.

If you're a woman with a sex addiction, you've got it made. Simply hang out at skeevy bars and sleep with every guy who asks. After you have sex, make sure you feel guilty and ashamed. How could you do that sort of thing with a complete stranger? Don't you feel low? Dirty?

Unfortunately, sex can be fun. So if you slip and start enjoying this addiction, carry a Bible with you. Read the passages aloud about being burned in hell for promiscuity. Believe them.

If you don't believe in God, there are many other ways to punish yourself for having sex. Explore them. Be creative. Go to any length to hurt yourself.

Remember, to be a good addict, you must think of nothing else but your addiction. It must consume all your thoughts. It must cost you everything. Your loved ones, your dignity and nearly your life.

So find one and work hard, your life will be in tatters before you know it. The pain of addiction will be more fun than you can possibly imagine! What a great way to spend your life and your life savings! Unimaginable pleasure!

Worksheet For Step Ten:

1. According to the experts, binge drinking is four or more drinks for women, five or more for men at a single sitting. Last night you had four drinks with the girls. Are you at the beginning stages of an addiction?

2. You smoked an ounce of weed, drank a fifth of Jack Daniels and snorted two grams of cocaine before you plowed your car into the garage and ruined your new boat. Your wife wants you to get into some kind of counseling for your drug use. Should you?

3. Every time you try to drink more than five or six drinks you throw up. What is wrong with you?

4. You can't afford cocaine, but really want to be addicted to something. Everything seems so expensive. What should you do?

5. You spent every last cent on the roulette wheel and have no money left to pay your child support. Do you get three jobs to pay the support and meet your financial commitments? Or do you take a second mortgage out on your house and turn it into millions at the craps tables?

Answers:

1. No. You wimp. Four drinks? That's all. Come on, girl. You're going to have to try harder than that. Try two six packs. Those statistics are so dumb. Binge drinking is for wusses. You want alcoholism, okay? Not some pansy ass binge drinking. Moron.

2. Who the hell are you married to? Mrs. Goody Two Shoes? Where did you pick up that loser? Counseling? Are you nuts? You're just getting the hang of the self-destructive racket. What you need to do is to divorce that wife of yours and spend every last cent on drugs and alcohol. And congratulations on crashing into your new boat. I hope you didn't have insurance on it.

3. You picked the wrong drug, stupid. Try cocaine. And if that makes you throw up, try heroin. But then again, that is sure to make you throw up. You may just have to turn to sex for an addiction. I sure as hell hope that doesn't make you throw up.

4. You obviously weren't reading my chapter very closely. Go back and read the methamphetamines section again. This is cheap and little goes a long way. And if you're poor, why aren't you on welfare? Or just steal the money from a relative, you loser. It doesn't cost that much to be addicted to meth. And the results will be so disastrous, you won't believe how bad your life can be. Enjoy!

5. You freakin' moron. Isn't it obvious? Take the damn mortgage out on the stupid house. What are you, a wuss? No, you're a winner, you just haven't hit it yet. The

next one is the big one. The big payoff. Mortgage yourself to the hilt—big wins take big stakes. And when you lose everything, including your dignity, you'll have me to thank.

Are you in jail and suffering from withdrawals yet? Facing bankruptcy? Haven't slept in seventeen days and look like a living skeleton? Has your spouse left you? Is your life in shambles? Great.

You should be so proud of yourself by now. Your life must really suck. Not only do you hate yourself, you're an addict, one of the biggest losers on this planet, everyone hates you, you're fat, you're ugly—all of which adds up to one thing: you have arrived! Congratulate yourself, you've won the game, you have hit rock bottom! Good job!

Conclusion

☙ 🜂 ❧

Well, you should now be the proud owner of one of the worst lives on the planet. I am very happy for you. Now you know true misery, the meaning of isolation, the depths of despair, the pit of loneliness. You know what it's like to be the butt of everyone's jokes. What it's like to be one of the most pitiful, despicable, hated individuals on God's green Earth.

Just think, no one can help you now. You are at the bottom. You are the crap that people scrape off their shoes before they go into their homes.

Basically, you have won the misery game. Isn't it wonderful? Isn't this the happiest you've ever been? Your life is the absolute pits! Such joy in misery!

You've worked so hard and what great rewards for all your efforts. No one is speaking to you, you're broke, your family has disowned you, you are unemployable, you're living in the streets, everyone shuns you, and your life totally sucks.

And you have me to thank for it. I know because my life sucks as much as yours does. Even worse, actually. Hey I wrote the book on it, didn't I?

But my life sucking is not the point here. The point is you. Now that you've completely destroyed your life, it is up to you to sustain this painful level of depression. It won't be easy. Chances are you're already thinking of reforming: kicking the addiction, losing the weight, apologizing to your mother-in-law, getting into therapy and cleaning up your life.

Take my advice and don't. No one likes people who succeed in life. Look at Bill Gates, he's got everything and everyone hates him.

Even if you attain the goals society wants you to have, you lose. No one wants anyone to be happy on this planet. That's why we pollute our environment, drink, eat tons of junk food, avoid voting, abuse our spouses and children and trap ourselves in jobs we hate. We don't want to be happy. We want our lives to suck.

So, give it up. Don't try to improve yourself, it won't pay off. Just enjoy your misery. Because remember, misery loves company. And even though you feel alone, you're not. You're among most of the humans on this planet. Only you had to work a lot harder to get here. Which should make you feel even more stupid and miserable. Which was the goal of this book. So, be happy, your life is ruined.

And now if you'll excuse me, my job is done here. I'm gonna go have a beer, eat a box of marshmallow pies and watch some TV...

Appendix A:
Negative Affirmations

CR 🖤 ƏO

Here are some extra negative affirmations to use when you start feeling good about yourself. See How To Use This Book in the beginning of the book for the proper technique on using these affirmations.

- *My nose belongs on Mount Rushmore.*

- *These orange prison coveralls make me look fat.*

- *A chainsaw is the only thing that would help my appearance.*

- *My husband/wife is starting to look like Rush Limbaugh.*

- *My butt looks like the Goodyear blimp.*

- *Some other homeless person is going to steal my street corner.*

- *I have the personality of a small soap dish.*

- *My cat is possessed by the spirit of Richard Nixon.*

- *My blind date will be Pauly Shore.*

- *I am starting to look like Tiny Tim.*

- *That second cake I just ate is going to make me fat.*

- *My defense attorney is sleeping with my wife.*

- *My breath smells like an elephant's butt.*

- *Barbie has more brains than I do.*

- *I am going to get a Chia Pet for Christmas..*

- *My feet are sooo ugly.*

- *Osama Bin Laden gets more chicks than I do.*

- *I am a toad.*

Appendix B:
Mental Tricks For
Staying Depressed

CЯ ☹ ഔ

You may need some help staying depressed. Below are some mental tricks to play on yourself to ensure your continued agony.

- *Think of past embarrassing moments and relive them.*

Remember that time you got into the hot tub naked with a group of friends because you thought everyone else was naked, but they weren't? You turned out to be the only naked person in the tub that night. To add insult to injury, your latest crush was there to witness your display and was turned off. You were completely humiliated.

Or what about that time you forgot to wash your hands after you used the hemorrhoid cream and then flossed your teeth? You got that nasty cream all over your teeth and jammed deep into your gums. Your teeth started getting all tingly and you were so freaked out you called poison control and they all laughed so hard, they accidentally hung up on you.

Or what about the time you had a booger on your nose during an entire date with a guy you had a crush on, but didn't find out why he was avoiding looking at you until you got home that night?

Or what about the time you got a woody in fifth grade and had to go up and answer a question in front of the whole class?

Or what about when you were talking about the boss's wife and she was standing right behind you?

Or what about the time you asked your friend when the baby was due and she wasn't pregnant, she had just gained weight?

Think of these awful times and let them repeat over and over and over in your mind. Weren't you the stupidest person on the planet? Didn't you feel humiliated? Don't you still now, even to this day, feel stupid even though it's been years since the event?

Allow yourself to relish these feelings. Dwell on them.

You really are still a dork. You know that, don't you?

• *Think of your past mistakes.*

The really bad ones. Allow yourself to steep in the humiliation of them. Here are some examples:

Your first, second and third husbands.

When you got caught embezzling from the snack bar in high school.

When your mother found out you cheated on the Bar exam.

The time you got that girl pregnant, her father found out and came after you with a shotgun.

The time you lied about your past education to get that job and the girl you started dating from the office found out, told the boss and he humiliated you as he fired you in front of all the other employees.

The time you accidentally slept with your best friend's husband.

The time you repeated something someone told you in confidence at a friend's wedding, which caused a huge fight that the bride had to break up, and she ended up getting punched in the process. And then everyone found out your big mouth was the cause of the whole mess.

The time a friend of yours got you that summer job at a store and you got caught stealing and your friend had to fire you.

The time when you were sixteen and you got your five-year-old brother stoned.

The time you were working for the state park and you rode the tractor too close to the edge of a cliff and it started to go over and all you could do was jump off and watch it go. And then you lied about it to your superiors, got caught and were fired.

Or what about the time when you were twelve and were reading girlie magazines under your sister's bed (because you were afraid of getting caught under your own) and you were using a Bic lighter instead of a flashlight (because you were stupid) and you caught her bed on fire and nearly burned down the entire house?

Now go over and over and over these memories and make them fresh again. Don't you feel stupid? Why couldn't you have stopped yourself from making such obvious mistakes? So what if you were young, what was wrong with you? You certainly have no excuses for the trouble you caused later in life. Don't you wish you could go back and undo the damage you caused to yourself and others? Well, you can't. Those were your mistakes, live with them. Hourly. Never let them go. Make it seem as if they happened yesterday and punish yourself for them.

Repeat the following over and over in your head: *stupid, stupid, stupid* while smacking yourself with something. This should make you feel bad. Which is good. Remember, any time you let yourself slip and get happy, there are many ways to bring yourself down. Past mistakes will never go away. Well, only if you get Alzheimer's. But I don't recommend that because misery is best enjoyed while fully conscious.

About The Author

C8 ☠ 80

Janet Periat was unfortunate enough to be born in California. This should explain everything that is wrong with her. But it doesn't. She lives a horrible life in an overpriced suburban wasteland. She is married to a guy who treats her well just to irritate her. She has one smelly, foul and evil cat. In her spare time, she falls off her new scooter, swears, drinks and watches television. You don't want to know this woman.

This page intentionally left blank.

Except for the previous statement. And this bit. Dammit! Now the page isn't blank anymore. My intentions have been thwarted.

My life sucks.